THE NORMANS ARE LANDING!

Hastings, 14th October 1066

Pierre EFRATAS and Gilles PIVARD

THE NORMANS ARE LANDING!

Hastings,
14th October 1066

OREP
EDITIONS

Zone tertiaire de Nonant – 14400 BAYEUX
Tel.: 02 31 51 81 31 – **Fax:** 02 31 51 81 32
info@orepeditions.com – www.orepeditions.com

Editor: Grégory PIQUE
Conception design: OREP
Graphics and Layout: Sophie YOUF
Editorial coordination: Corine DESPREZ
English translation: Heather INGLIS

Wooden swords, steel swords

I've always been afraid of the dark. Probably because of what my grandmother used to tell me when I was 4.

"You know, Arnoul, sometimes dark spirits swallow up living beings. The next morning, after searching and searching, all that's left is blood and crushed bones."

Charming story. It was dark, I was 15, and I was afraid.

Yet, I was not alone: there were fifty of us, sitting on chest benches, dressed as warriors. Boiled leather breastplates or overalls garnished with metal rings, hauberks[1] and puttees were what comprised our accoutrements. Placed either next to us or inside chests, there was an array of conical nasal helmets, axes, swords and long painted wooden shields.

The long boat's coppery bow was sparkling under the flickering flame of a flare attached to the top of the mast. The sea was breathing like

---

1. Medieval coat of arms

a dragon ready to devour us. Across the vague waves, under the sniggering clouds, dozens, hundreds of steeds of the waves thrust forward north-westerly, their lanterns trembling in the wind. Straight towards England.

"Tomorrow," Count Boselin, a bald giant exclaimed as he leaned on the mast, "the Englisc and their perfidious king will learn to keep their word!"

"Haro[2]!" he cried with all his might.

"Haro!"

We screamed as if we were possessed. And what a relief it was. I forgot my fear and that darned seasickness was regularly propelling my head overboard to evacuate the sour liquid that was wrenching my stomach.

"Haro!"

Many rough and scornful voices cried back from other boats. Like spectres that suddenly loomed from the waters.

My dear village of Dives, I miss you so! And I miss you too my mother, my father and my two stupid brothers! And you, Mahaut, my sweetheart, with your snowy smile and long brown hair! And you Toutain, my faithful companion...!

I shuddered as I recalled the events that had led to me joining this mad adventure, several

---

2. A cry used for hunting, warning, anger, indignation.

months before the night of the twenty-eighth to the twenty-ninth of September in the year of grace 1066.

*

It was a sunny fourth of April the same year; life was beautiful and the seagulls were dancing above the thatched roofs of our small village. Had you told me, at that precise instant, that I, Arnoul le Roux, son of lady Bérengère and Renouf Jambe Torte, a master carpenter in Dives, would find myself enlisted, driven and boarded for a horrifying military campaign in the company of eight thousand warriors, two thousand sailors, craftsmen, work hands and grooms, together with two thousand five hundred horses, boarded onto around a thousand ships, I would have told you you had gone mad.

Yet, that very day, my fate was to take a new turn.

Let me tell you.

My friend Toutain and I simply loved tussling just for fun. It had never gone much further – even if, one day, that idiot almost broke my nose, making it bleed profusely. Toutain called me Sire Squirrel, for – I must admit – I'm not particularly tall, even if I'm very muscular, I have a short nose, big hazelnut eyes, even bigger feet and an extraordinary sense of balance! In turn, I called my friend "Lord Loud Mouth" because, as voices go, that blond-haired giant's is a pretty thunderous one.

At the top of the hill, on the forest's edge, we set up a small enclosed field. An old rope and four pegs outlined the corners and the sides. We took up position on either side of the field. And off we went! Laughing all along – I know that's rather stupid but you must admit that stupid things are generally what make you laugh – we pounced on each other, howling, proudly brandishing our light wooden swords, axes and shields. Take that! Filaments of cinder flickered in the air as wood blew against wood in a deafening clash. We parried, jumped, turned, we lunged and defended as if our lives depended on it. It gradually became an increasingly complex dance.

When our chainsils[3] were soaked in sweat, one of us decided to fall, in a cry of agony. And the battle was over! We were shattered, but I can guarantee it's the best way to let off steam after a day's wood chopping. We then headed home, where a different ceremony began. My mother always shrieked at the sight of my clothes, whilst my father sniggered and my brothers tittle tattled. And I headed straight

---

3. Men's and women's overgarment.

for the bath tub...

So there I was, late afternoon on St. Isidore's day, waiting for Loud Mouth at the top of the hill. Toutain was always late. The pegs were in place, the ropes tautened and I was busy swivelling "Ripper" my sword.

"Who do you think you are?" whined a far too familiar voice.

I turned round. No mistake. Stick in hand, Robert and his two brothers had come to pick a quarrel. Those three were the Trinity of horror. Robert, a small boy with a squint nose, who smelled like a dead cow. Foulque, a tall, pale-eyed cretin who spent his time spitting on the ground. And Gernot, as red as bad wine, who flapped his disproportionately long arms. The poor guy is so simple that I'm sure he knows no more than twenty words, including: "Can you see my fist? Can you see your head? Can you see the connection?"

"He thinks he's a hero," Robert persisted, "but he's no more than a thief's son..."

"Who's doing just like his father," added Gernot (sorry, he knows six more words).

"And who's going to pay for it," Foulque gravely concluded.

No point in trying to negotiate with those three morons, in trying to tell them that just because our fathers are at loggerheads doesn't mean we need to come to blows. They moved forward with a malicious smile, tapping their sticks on the palms of their hands. I had, of course, already been known to give Gernot a good thrashing. But at one against three, and with my dummy weapons, I was in a tricky situation. By the grace of God! Protected by my small round shield and my short sword, I stood up to them.

My heart was in my boots. But when Robert said my mother was a - well, let's not go there - I was engulfed by a surge of hatred. A red veil covered my eyes. Everything strangely seemed to be in slow motion. Through the curtain of my wrath, I could distinguish every one of my gestures. Hardened. I was numb. I fought. Sticks flew in all directions...

... Suddenly, silence. A flock of firebirds took flight in a flurry of feathers.

"Well done!"

An ironic voice and applause brought me back to reality. I could see a tall and scarfaced knight wearing a blue bliaud[4], a red cape fastened at the shoulder with a golden hook and grey woollen hat adorned with a ruby red feather. A dozen other knights, obviously of lesser importance, were standing behind him. They all seemed quite amused.

---

4. Fine linen or hemp tunic, generally worn as an undergarment.

The blue bliaud then continued, in a knowledgeable tone,

"Let's see: cut, thrust, feint[5] and bam! Three men to the ground. By the heavenly king, I declare that is pure poetry in motion!"

His companions approved. As if I had just been saved from drowning, I finally gazed around me. The three brothers were in a sorry state. To greet the visitor, they took to their knees, groaning.

"He's Count Boselin," they mumbled with terror.

"Can you hear me talking to you?" Boselin asked me. "I asked you your name."

In turn, I took to my knees. And I could believe neither my mouth nor my ears...

---

5. To cut consists in hitting with the side of the sword's blade, thrust with the tip and feint is a simulated sword move to trick the adversary or to make him move in a desired direction.

The new recruit

"And you accepted!" my father exploded, his grey moustache bristling like a cat's whiskers. "You have joined up with that swashbuckler Boselin at a time when war is on everyone's lips! You crazy clot! Have I not already told you about the Varaville massacre, when I fought for Duke William? Have you seen the state of my leg? That's what being a soldier is all about!"

"Father, if you'd stayed with him, you wouldn't be ruining your health and we would be eating something better than soup and bread all week long."

"Renouf, stop!" my mother cried as she held back the (heavy) hand of my progenitor, ready to set my cheek ablaze.

With her hands on her hips, her tousled blond hair hanging round her shoulders, my mother defied the great Renouf, who, despite his limp, was still a fearsome man.

"If Arnoul wants to try his luck," she said, extremely irritated, "if he wants to earn a decent living, and perhaps even recognition from Boselin and respect from all, you can't stop him."

"A decent living," sighed my father as he shrugged his shoulders. "Respect. Recognition... If that's what you think," he added, with a weary look, his deep blue eyes suddenly dampening, "then prepare yourself for a disappointment. War stinks of filth, blood and suffering. Sometimes it can hurt you, break you and turn you into a source of pity for the rest of your life. Or better still: a kind-hearted but dislocated cadaver thrown into a soon forgotten ditch."

"I've heard enough!"

"Arnoul! Where are you going?" asked my mother as she tried to hold me back.

"Outside. I need some fresh air."

I slammed the door and quickly crossed the narrow street lined with cob and half-timbered facades. Night had fallen over Dives and the sky glistened with sparkling jewels. In the distance, I could hear the tide rising. With a heavy heart, I sat on the flat stone that marks the edge of the village. It was my favourite spot for admiring the starry vault.

Tip-tap, tip-tap, I heard footsteps: it was Mahaut, my little elf, her long brown hair gleaming with a stellar glow. "Hurry, I must tell you..."

"Don't say a word," she whispered as she sat down beside me. "I know everything. We'll talk about that tomorrow."

Mahaut took my hand and coiled her head under my neck. Then,

"Arnoul, do you think you can read the future in the stars?"

"I don't know. But if you were my star, it would be a gentle one."

My brunette laughed. We kissed. Yet, a strange anguish was tormenting me, a deaf and cold anguish. From now on, I knew that fear would be my companion.

*

As arranged, ten days later, I headed for Count Boselin's fortified house, located on top of the hill that looms above the Dives estuary. My heart was beating like a hundred swords on their shields. After giving the two steel-clad sentries the password, I crossed the bridge above the ditch, then the wooden stockade and I walked across the courtyard where a dozen soldiers were training with their spears and swords. I took the stairs. I entered a dark room, illuminated only by a crackling girandole[6].

"Ah. Our valiant lawman," Boselin said as he raised his bald and scarred head.

He scrutinised me from behind his small table. Then he fixed his gaze on my sword.

"Chopper" he enquired.

---

6. Chandelier with several branches.

"Yes, sire."

"Take great care of it. Your father's sword has slain many a courageous man."

"And now," he added, with a harsher look, "listen to me carefully. The decision has been made: we are going to cross the sea and make war with the Englisc king. Do you still want to fight by my side? If you retract, I won't hold it against you."

What a question! I had always loved flirting with danger. Climbing up trees. Doing balancing acts on old walls. Running through a storm. It's no surprise, with my small size, the colour of my hair and my funny little ways, that they call me the Squirrel.

"No retraction, sire."

"Good," Boselin approved. "You have a sense of honour and a brave heart – not forgetting your fighting skills. But that's not enough to be a good soldier.

From now on, the only privileges you will be granted are the right to sigh, sweat and perhaps regret your pledge.

But, tis of no great concern to me. The day we leave, you must be a rock among rocks. The Englisc, the Saxons in particular, are the best of Christian soldiers. To crush them, we will need a mountain of strength."

Boselin stood up and headed for the door.

"Turgis," he cried, "a new recruit!"

An omen?

On the twenty-fourth of April, the sky was illuminated by a strange fire, as livid as death itself. It was a comet that blazed for several days and several nights. White flame, what news do you bring: victory or disaster?

When will we leave?

Sweat! Sigh! Smell like an old dog's ass! The icy wind bit into my shaved neck – I hated my regulation haircut. Exercise! Fatigue duty! Along with my companions in misfortune, Godfré the Long and Frowin Heavybelly, we transported tubs of sewage into a low ditch pending the installation of latrines on the vast plateau that was to be used as a camp. We then helped the work hands to carry heavy stakes and stones. Mounds of stones. My arms and my legs cried out for pity, but Turgis was already barking at us.

"Training! Take up your weapons. Quick. The last one to arrive will run down and back up the hill."

Such were my daily occupations. And even if that bulldog Turgis treated me worse than a doormat, he taught me a lot. For although I am a good runner and a proficient swordsman, my command of the spear is atrocious and my archery skills unspeakable. As for my small size and my far too light weight, I must compensate with my steel muscles and excellent posture, otherwise I would be swept away like an autumn leave. I was to realise to my expense that Sire Bulldog was right.

*

"Into battle!"
Barely at cockcrow, in line, we thrust forward onto another line of soldiers, brandishing our shields and taking care to avoid theirs. It was tough work. My entire body was throbbing. The impact sent stars sparkling through my eyes. At each assault, I reeled. Then all of a sudden...

...I found myself lying amidst the dust. Someone helped me up. A nobleman, judging by his attire and the way he held his head.

"Lad, you're not placing your feet properly. Once you've learned how to place your feet, you'll be ready."

My head was turning and my heart full of shame. I failed to hold back a nervous laugh.

"Why are you laughing?" (His dark eyes were now as cutting as knives).

"Er... to mock my foolishness, sire."

Wrong answer. Black Eye grabbed me by the collar and, with his angular face just an inch from mine, he bellowed,

"If you're not fond of yourself, death is simply going to adore you. You must be strong and proud on the battlefield. A ferocious lion. Got it, lad?"

"With all due respect, Sire Robert", the Bulldog intervened, in a surprisingly gentle tone, "I'd like to look after this idiot myself."

"On you go," Black Eye ordered, "and never forget what I told you. Strong body, agile feet."

I had just encountered Roger de Montgomerie, one of Duke William's powerful lords who had taken command of the camp and who was preparing to gather our army. But I had little time to enquire. I got two days' fatigue duty for chattering during exercises.

*

Turgis was not as bad a chap as I had thought. On the ninth of May, he gave me three days' leave, telling me that, perhaps, he could make something similar to a soldier out of me. (Incredible: on his craggy face, I could almost make out something that vaguely resembled a smile).

"By the fangs of a wild dog!" he howled as he spat on the ground. "Stop looking at me like a fried squirrel and get out of here before I change my mind. Out with you!"

When I arrived home, my mother covered me with kisses as if I had escaped from a dragon's jaws. When they saw my haircut, my brothers guffawed and my father told me I smelled of the army and that the water tub would do me the world of good. At that precise instant, my friend Toutain turned up, covered in dust. He shook me like an apple tree in autumn. "Knight! You're a knight! I knew it!" (Loud Mouth was always generous as far as exaggeration goes).

*

When I returned, clean and dry, my father told me with a frown that he had been requisitioned to build boats in the harbour in Dives. And in a defiant tone,

"Tell me, hot head, do you at least know why you're going to fight?"

"Of course I do. One, day, old King Edward sent Harold Godwinson (an important Saxon lord) with a message for William, "Duke, when death shalt be mine, my crown shalt be yours." The Saxon crossed the channel and passed on the message. Then the two lords waged war against Breton rebels; they became good friends. Before heading back to England, Harold swore an oath of allegiance to our duke on holy relics. However, when Edward died, the traitor broke his word and had himself crowned king! With God's help, we are going to make him pay for his treachery!"

"Leave our good God alone," my father sneered, "for here's your goddess."

Mahaut was watching me from the doorway, as touching as ever. And the big ninny I am started crying with joy.

Forward march!

It was August. The lazy clouds drifted under a gentle breeze. Warriors came from all around. From all four corners of the duchy, of course, but also from Brittany, Flanders, Picardy, Poitou, Maine, Anjou and from the kingdom of the Franci[7]. The Normans of Sicily, Calabria and Apulia crossed the sea and the mountains, travelling thousands of miles to join forces with Duke William. From Dives, below, on the banks of the gulf that stretch out as far as Troarn, we could see an immense shambles of horses, cattle-drawn carts, armed horsemen, foot soldiers, crossbowmen, archers, seamen and peasants bringing meat and flour. The waters overflowed with ships, many of them warships, streamlined, their huge sails swollen with the wind, their bows carved with characters and monsters of all sorts. Others were fishing or trading boats.

Up on our hilltop, and across a surface area of a hundred hectares, Roger de Montgomerie's vast camp was gradually covered with tents. A

---

7. People of France

thousand, in no time. Further away, around three thousand small horses frolicked in the neighbouring enclosures and prairies where a myriad of grooms were hard at work.

Our training period was now over. Godfré and I were enlisted in the infantry, under Boselin's direct orders. The Bulldog had just informed us, adding for my personal attention,

"You have qualities, Squirrel, I can't say the contrary. But when you see the Saxons, try not to stain your braccae[8]." (Turgis laughed to himself. Adopting a composed pace, he headed for Montgomerie's guard where his sense of humour and his distinction worked wonders).

Otherwise, I met with Gwenaël, a Breton who was as blond as he was tall and slim, and Erwin, a Flemish giant who was always laughing and singing. We got together sometimes in the evening with Godfré and Taillefer, a small and stocky chap with a broken nose, who appreciated our good spirits and who was liked by all (in particular by the constable Hugues de Montfort, which proved quite useful). Taillefer knew some astonishing stories and recited poetry. To the sound of a penny whistle, he recited the Song of Roland. Many flocked around him to listen and applause.

---

8. Ancient, then medieval garment similar to trousers or leggings, that could be loose-fitting or not.

When the time came to sleep and I found myself on my bed of hay, it was no longer laughter that abounded, but anguish that murmured, in my grandmother's voice, terrible stories of ancestors who had travelled the icy seas in their longboats. A huge snake emerged from the waters, overturning an entire fleet, whilst thunder struck the dark mountains, rolling their rocks, and in battles where fire rose to the skies, spears reddened and raised axes were torn apart.

Sometimes I must admit, and even regret, my own temerity. Am I truly of the stuff to be rubbing shoulders with these soldiers whose faces bear the traces of years of combat? Or am I mad, like my father claims?

Instantly, Mahaut appeared in my dreams, her brown hair standing on end,

"That's enough! No moaning allowed! If you come back victorious, I will be the proudest woman of all Normandy. And should you die, I will cherish your name my whole life over."

Decidedly, my dearest Mahaut always finds the right words to make you feel better. I should logically have felt an icy chill run down my spine... But no: instead I laughed to myself and fell asleep.

*

There they were! Duke William and the papal banner had arrived! A wave of enthusiasm swept across the entire camp. As he led his impressive army, we could see him at last – the one we all wanted to see crowned King of England. Mounted on a black horse, the duke left me awestruck. Not because he was tall, our William, but because of the determination that glistened in his grey eyes, his hostile expression, his mouth, deliberately indented with a short nose and a powerful chin, conveying a rare strength of character. What's more, he was a redhead, like me!

Cheers burst out all around. When he arrived in the middle of the camp, Turstin Fitz Rollo, who was carrying the papal banner, moved away from the group and took three steps forward. The duke raised his arm. Then Odo, the bishop of Bayeux, blessed us. We placed one knee on the ground. Soon, all we could hear were the cries of the seagulls and the song of the wind through the forest. Then the bishop's voice resounded, clear and determined. "Victory," he affirmed, "will be ours, for God punishes usurpers." I don't know why, but my progenitor's voice echoed in my head, "Arnoul, leave God alone! Just try to stay alive."

*

When were we going to leave? Fifteen times over these long weeks, we had travelled down to the shoreline to train in embarking and landing. The first time was a disaster. The great lengths deployed by Hugues de Montfort and the roaring orders given by Roger de Montgomerie, Eustace of Boulogne, Hamon de Creully, William FitzOsbern and Alan Rufus, were of no use. Several men fell into the sea, some of them even drowned, and since the operations proved too time-consuming, the rising tide prevented a third of the army from boarding their ships.

The duke was furious. On his palfrey, he galloped across the beaches and the shoreline bellowing with anger.

"Sottas! Hnoc[9]! Wake up! Be warned, we'll start over and over again until your bellies are full of sand."

William kept his word. The next day, second exercise. The following day, third exercise, and henceforth, until the ninth day when things started to change. The ships were perfectly stabilised with blocks placed under their hulls; the wooden walkways were in place on their planking; foot soldiers, horses and grooms embarked and disembarked in a perfectly orderly fashion. At the thirteenth attempt –

---

9. Fools! Simpletons!

27

besides a few lazybones who were promised fitting reprisal – the army embarked in less than six hours. This time, we were bestowed with congratulations from Duke William and his constable. To reward us, the next day we were allowed to rest, and to feast. And the following day, for a change of scenery, we were granted a melee – the fifth of its kind. An exercise I simply love, and as you'll see, it loves me back.

No mercy

What could be more exciting than a melee!? It's as easy as pie, even if it takes a little time: the army is split into two troops ready to challenge each other. The rules are a little more complicated. The infantrymen and the horsemen are allowed to strike, push and press their adversary, but at the same time, they must absolutely restrain their blows and avoid injuring. The archers and crossbowmen manoeuvre with us – but without firing, an exercise for which they will, of course, have other opportunities. The general aim is to learn to act together as a group and to check how each individual strength can serve the group strength. "Don't forget," the constable frequently proclaimed, "that the strength of the chain is that of its weakest link."

To start with, we organised ourselves according to our battle chiefs' instructions. The duke lowered his rod of command. Trumpets resounded. The exercise began. Turn round! Retreat! Advance! Fast!" Faster! Stop!... And we waited, standing under the stifling sun or torrential rain, without being allowed to move an inch.

Other times, we slowly progressed towards each other, in the most perfect order possible. Then it was time to charge. United like one single warrior, in an immense metal porcupine, the earth trembled under our feet. Forward march for the melee! The infantrymen tapped their shields as the horsemen simulated retreats. And that's when certain bits of advice had a real effect on me. My feet correctly positioned, my body straight and taut, I turned and twirled, I lunged and I plunged. Much to my surprise, five of my adversaries yielded, groaned and fell. Embarrassed, I helped them get up, but, rather than insulting me, they shook me and laughed. "Well done kid!" yelled a giant who seemed delighted with his fall. "You can pay us a round in England!"

"Hey you! That's enough, Squirrel!" Boselin cried, "We're not here for a laugh! Withdraw!" Once back at the camp, I was expecting to be reprimanded, for I had overstepped the order which consisted in pushing our adversaries, but not making them fall. And it was quick in coming: Count Boselin summoned me to his tent.

"Gadzooks!" he screamed in my ears. What came over you Squirrel?"

— ...

After which, believe it or not, he burst out laughing, gave me a hug and confessed that, thanks to me, he had been congratulated by Seigneur Montgomerie.

"To punish you," he continued, resuming a severe tone, "tomorrow, at dawn, you will go to the harbour, where you will wait for Mora, our duke's ship. As soon as it arrives, you will ask for Étienne Einard and you will bring him here." Then he added in a whisper,

"Since the ship is only due to arrive in the afternoon, if you go and see your family, I may well turn a blind eye."

*

It was chilly on the shore. The wind was refusing to blow from the west and was stirring up small puffs of sand. Sheltered by the dune, my father and his apprentice carpenters (including my good friend Toutain who still thought I was a paladin[10]) were gazing at a boat they had tarred and repainted urgently.

"Well now!" I said with a laugh, "With that darned wind coming from the wrong direction, it doesn't look like we'll be leaving today."

What had I dared to say? My short-tempered father stood up and, pointing his finger at me, "Because you believe all that hogwash! If William breathes in the wind, it's not to check

---

10. Elite horseman.

its direction, it's to sense the perfect moment to surprise his prey. He's always done that. So, before opening your mouth, try to think a bit!" I was preparing a sharp rejoinder when a magnificent ship entered the harbour. On the bow – and not on the stern as usual – gleamed the statue of a child dressed in gold. His right arm was pointing out towards the high seas and his left arm held an ivory horn to his mouth. The ducal colours flapped at the top of the mast.

"I believe that's your Mora," my father said. "We'll catch up later."

To my ignorance, they were to be the last words he would say to me before I left.

As for the famous, or rather woolly Étienne Einard who was waiting for me at the harbour, tapping his foot... well he's only worth a few words. The steersman of William's ship looked me up and down from his high mountain of pretentiousness. Not a greeting, not a word, apart from asking me, his nose turned up, if the camp was far.

Once we reached our destination His Haughtiness turned on his heels without even murmuring those horrible words "thank you", much likely to skin his lips. I hastened to forget about him: throughout the camp, the word spread of our imminent departure. It was the eighth of September...

The waves of war

William had stopped breathing in the wind. On the eleventh of September, a westerly breeze rose at last and we gathered up all our strength and embarked. But not for the kingdom of the Englisc: for Saint-Valéry, in the Bay of Somme.

Across the raging sea, for ten horrific hours, from violent gusts to icy waves, from dizziness to seasickness, we sailed for the very first time.

"Oyez Arnoul!"

We overtook a slower boat from which Gwenaël was waving energetically to me.

"Oyez Arnoul, can't you hear me?"

Well, try to answer with your head streaming with salty water, your mouth dribbling with acidy liquid! It was even harder to answer three days later when, under the pouring rain, Erwin told me our Breton friend's boat had sunk.

No! Not him...

My tears shed like a river. The howling wind stabbed me to the heart.

It rained incessantly for several days. I was up to my knees in mud, it was cold and every day seemed like an interminable ordeal. Thankfully, on the twenty-sixth of September, the weather turned dry. In the evening, I watched the stars, under the mocking gaze of some of my companions, who were mumbling that my beauty had turned me into a dofian[11]. Suddenly, my Flemish friend Erwin turned up and told anyone vaguely interested that Taillefer was about to sing.

"Stop dreaming and come and enjoy yourself!" he said to me, beaming and grabbing me by the arm.

Godfré took to his heels and we ran towards a high crackling bonfire.

*

I'm sure that Taillefer had never gathered so many spectators round his stories. It was said that this talented lyricist would tell us great secrets! Thus, a huge crowd gathered and if Godfré, Erwin and I hadn't been his good chums, we would never have elbowed our way through the thick lines of spectators, who were impatiently clapping their hands.

---

11. Doting fool.

Upright in front of the fire, his arms hanging the length of his body, impassive and silent, Taillefer stared at us like a cat stares at frogs frolicking in a pond. He finally deigned to open his mouth to ask us to hush. The buzz of the audience quietened, and the little fellow took to his penny whistle and began to sing,

Harold of the Englisc upon his steed
From the cliff top gazes out to sea
Waves of violence, winds of ice
Rapid clouds and angry skies
An empty horizon, no ducal fleet
The traitor plays, light-heartedly
"Tis not this year's fate!
The season's too late
To London, I can return
And my whole army adjourn!"
Harold of the Englisc, in his capital
Is awakened by the thunder
Falling like a weight from his pedestal:
Northern lands at war and plunder!
"The Norwegians are upon us
Like swarms of moths at nightfall
Warriors, unite in boldness
For we will crush them all!"

Upon these words, and without waiting to see if another verse remained to be sung, everyone rose and roared, "To England! To England!", and I was far from the last to cry out at the top of my voice. His arms crossed, his eyes sparkling more than blazing logs, Taillefer gazed at us with a contented smile. When the crowd had calmed down, he made us repeat the last three lines several times: "Like swarms of moths at nightfall, Warriors, unite in boldness, For we will crush them all!"

The duke, and the weather, must have heard us: at dawn on the twenty-eighth of September, the sky was cleared of the last clouds and the air turned mild thanks to a gentle southerly zephyr. The horns resounded throughout the camp. On your feet! The time for action has come! On that bright morning, our quivering, impatient army headed for the shoreline. In the distance, downstream, on the opposite bank of the Somme estuary, I was sure I could see my sweetheart's silhouette. But it was only a small tree from which birds were taking flight. Goodbye Mahaut, goodbye your fragrant kisses on my lips, goodbye my mother's embrace, my brothers' laughter, my father's rough but reassuring voice. Goodbye my dear friend Toutain. The time has come for the waves of adventure, and of war.

*

The day was long and the night was gruelling. Such was my lot on the boat that pitched high, sick among the sick, frozen, my head full of my grandmother's old psalmodies.

Hurry on, steed of the seas
Toss the water and split the breeze
Head straight on and drive ahead
For tomorrow's dawn will be bloodshed

"Hey! Squirrel! It's time to wake up. We'll soon be in England!"

Godfré shook me, overwhelmed by great excitement. My tongue coated, staggering, I dragged myself from the claws of slumber to finally see what awaited us: the English coast lined with long sandy beaches. In an impressive surge, our fleet advanced towards the wide bay. Upon Boselin's orders, we donned our helmets, shields, ring armour, spears and swords. Miracle: my seasickness had stopped. From now on, I wanted just one thing: to fight.

And we landed

No enemy, no battle. On the beach at Pevensey, our army landed without the slightest hitch. In turn, I set foot on the pale sand that crunched under my hose. Breath in, Arnoul, fill your lungs with this new air; here, you are no longer an apprentice, you are no longer the carpenter's lad, the kid who used to play with a wooden sword. Good God no! On this particular St. Michael's day, you have become a Norman, ready to wage war on English soil, a well-trained soldier perfectly aware of what he must do and when he must do it, and who has earned respect from his companions. Perhaps, if you had been in my shoes, you would have felt proud, sure that you were about to take part in an enterprise that would drastically transform the Christian world. Perhaps, like me, you would also have forgotten all those intoxicating great words and vainglory. For, as each instant passed by, as each manoeuvre was completed, from the towing of the boats onto the sand to our forward march, in ranks, across the dunes, I was stabbed with nostalgia, like a boat leaving the dock of its former life, forever.

*

We silently marched under the pitiless sun. A bitter snake of sweat wound its way from my forehead to my mouth, whilst others poured down my back with mocking sluggishness. By a cool wind and on flat terrain, the weight of my helmet, braccae and weapons seemed so much lighter than it had on that soft sandy hill my feet once sunk into. Then we reached a steep pitch overlooking the bay. Long stretches of water meandered through the forests, punctuated with a medley of hills and marshes. On the banks of one of these waterways stood a formidable grey-white stone enclosure, where our flag already proudly flew. "Waste no time!" cried the baron Hamon de Creully, positioned alongside our column, as he briskly rose up on his horse's spurs. "You'll have enough time to admire the walls once you're inside."

*

Inside the walls! He had a sense of humour Hamon. If we kept going at the same pace, I reckoned we wouldn't see them before the following day, and I was optimistic. Our army, our carts and our horses became entwined, entangled and cramped together before the vast gate of the fortress, defended by our vanguard. The ceremony of passwords was never-ending. We even noticed Harold's spies as they skedaddled[12] away. Alas, the impatient crowd outside was becoming increasingly angry, quarrelsome and particularly nasty with the guards. Inept they were, let me tell you! Chamber pots on legs, barely good enough to inflict misery on brave soldiers. The resulting din was such that the duke himself came to the wall. Just ten sharp words and the sentries could hear better, the army advanced and calm was restored... Relative calm, for, between the blackbirds' trill and the cawing of the rooks, a heavy wind brought snatches of bird cries and deaf groans. Soon another sound - that familiar crackling which, I know from experience, sends the forest residents into flight: the sound of flames as they devour wood. The smell of burning was quick to confirm my suspicions. Instinctively, I grabbed onto the pommel of Chopper, my sword.

A reaction that aroused the attention of Ditbert, a guy from Rouen with a husky voice and for whom war was as natural as the long purple nose on his face.

_____

12. Quickly sneak away.

"Stop being cruel to yourself, Squirrel. If you get edgy every time we burn an Englisc flea pit, you're not out of the woods, let me tell you."

I faked approval, for once Ditbert has you in the firing line, you're reputation's sealed, and in no way did I want to be considered a weakling.

"How do you think your pittance comes?" he continued. "People don't particularly like having their cows, sheep and hens pinched. And when they start telling you so, that's when things get dangerous. The best bet is to avoid snags like that and to show them who's boss."

A shadow was shed above us. We walked through the gateway that had been sneering at us for hours. Ditbert gave me a thump,

"Think about tonight's repast, and you'll get your wit back."

Always on guard

I think I was wrong to look that yellowbelly Einard up and down. I was carrying a box of rivets when I came across him, with his chalky face and constipated mouth. And wham! A true Arnoul-style look and you're in for a good bout of the runs. His Majesty Steersman the First, King of the Seas, became as red as a beacon. As I walked past him, I could sense his eyes burning my back like a branding iron. That very evening, I was told I would be wall sentry for ten nights over. And at the worst spot, of course: at the very top of the wooden keep that the duke had had built in the middle of an abandoned Saxon fort. Although the pieces of wood it was made from had been calculated, shaped, cut and positioned with rare scientific accuracy and in a timescale that would be the envy of any self-respecting horde of ants, when the wind blew up there, you really felt alive. It was as if we were on an unsteady ford threatened by the current. Just perfect for me, no?

At first, I grit my teeth, grabbed on to the wooden crenel with my right hand as I squeezed my spear with the left until my knuckles were white. That was how I managed to escape fainting. Since my neighbour was a Manceau[13] natterbox called Julien, I had no choice but to nonchalantly open my mouth from time to time. And thanks to his prattling, I eventually felt much better.

"For the love of God! Shut your trap!" groaned the third guard, brandishing what was left of his chipped teeth crowned with two sharply pointed canines.

"We're here to keep guard, not to chinwag all night," he added as he spat on the ground.

May God's grace be with you, Fly Trap! Thanks to your miraculous intervention, I could enjoy the night. Having said that, "enjoy" was rather optimistic. Distant blazes reddened the darkness all around the fortress. Sometimes, the flames tore through the silver shroud of bleak stars. To the east, we could see the outline of a small village on the edge of the forest, reduced to cinders. To the septentrion[14], a virtually collapsed stable smouldered amidst a deserted pasture. To the west, a far-stretching indented glow emerged from the horizon. Very probably a city, or a fortification.

---

13. Inhabitant of the town of Le Mans.

14. North.

"May God protect us from the Norman fury!" My grandmother's voice resounded in my head. She appeared before me, pale with glowing eyeballs. But this time, I was no longer a child scared by an old tale; this time, the Norman invader was me. And if the Englisc knew that my only fury was that of doubts and questions, they would probably die laughing.

*

Down our way, we say, "Inside the body of bad tidings, lies the heart of better news." The heart? No more guard duty on this blasted keep! (Aah). The body? To re-embark immediately! (Ooh).

Over a slack sea, we crossed the bay. After sailing alongside a bushy stretch of land, we reached a second bay. To the right perched on an escarpment overlooking the small harbour, stood a second wooden tower. We could see hundreds of men busy completing a wide stockade surrounded by a ditch and an embankment. Godfré already knew the name of this place: Hastings. How could we have guessed that it would remain perpetually engraved in the memories of men to come?

*

Back up to the top of a tower. Once more, I was on guard duty with Ditbert and the, now inevitable, Manceau. The night had already spilled forth half of its dark ink when Ditbert drew closer.

"I'm quite fond of you, Squirrel. So, from now on, open up your little ears. First of all: never believe the first rumour you hear. If you get word of a decimated Saxon army on its way down towards us, then interpret that as men who have just crushed a huge army led by Harald Hardrada, the King of Norway, the greatest fighter of our time. Secondly, if you hear anyone claim that Harold's a coward, you're allowed to slap your thighs with laughter. I saw the same customer fight at the Mont Saint-Michel and I can tell you, that guy's got nerve. Thirdly: if anyone tells you our duke fell in the sand when he landed, it's true. But he said it was because he wanted to hold his kingdom in his hands. Never forget that William is one of those strapping fellows that always get up again. Do you want an example? The day before yesterday, twenty-five of our horsemen got stuck in the marshes. He helped them out, and as if that weren't enough, he carried FitzOsbern's armour, as well as his own. Fourthly: nothing is ever sure, apart from the thrust you put behind your sword. So stop fretting. Fight with all your might and

you'll have a chance to know what the future holds. Got it?"
"Got it!"
We shook hands. Dawn broke over Hastings.

To arms!

"Monk, advise William to leave England."

"Monk, you'd better advise Harold to abandon his crown."

"Monk, tell Robert's son that my answer is no. I will continue my march towards victory."

"Monk, advise Godwin's son to go the stockade, where I shall defy him in a singular duel."

"Monk, reply to that duke that the Lord shall decide on the just outcome between him and me."

End of negotiations. The monk came back to William messageless, and the war became inevitable. Too bad for Harold, and his arrogance. Our walls were sure to shatter them both.

"Our walls!" Ditbert spluttered. "If we follow your stupid idea, we'll be surrounded in no time by more and more Englisc troops. I'll bet on my five scars that we'll soon be marching into battle. So, now's the time to say your prayers and confess your sins."

*

The night of the thirteenth of October lurked threateningly, as the horn wailed, "The Englisc are at the 'Grey Apple Tree'! To arms!"
Our army gathered at the foot of the keep to listen to the duke. Daring, justice, pride, his words were forceful, his tone clear and concise. Our ovation hit the skies. After Bishop Odo had celebrated Mass, praying to God to grant us victory, the time came to salute our companions and friends. Taillefer pinched my cheek, Ditbert embraced me like a son, Godfré, Erwin and I fell into each other's arms, Boselin ordered me not to disappoint him.
It was time to forget regrets and questions. And it was time for me to fight and, perhaps, to survive.

*

Forward march!
March, the Norman army, across plain and thicket, over hill and high grass. March till morning. One more hurdle to climb... And then...!

The battle

There, looming at a height of around 130 feet and on a plateau a good few hundred feet wide called Senlac, stood a fortress even more formidable than the ones we had seen in Pevensey and Hastings.

It was Harold's army, a continuous wall of thousands of shields lined up in several rows. In the midst of this monster, glistening with huge Danish axes, two standards flapped in the wind. The first represented a warrior, and the second a dragon. The flanks of this immobile, terrifying and deadly beast bristling with javelins were reinforced with other lines of thousands of motley infantrymen. A tangible vibration of merciless hatred emanated from each and every one of those silent ranks.

We took up position on the plain: the Normans in the centre, Bretons, Manceaux, Angevins, Poitevins[15] on the left wing, Flemish, Franci and Picards on the right. With our two thousand five hundred horsemen, five thousand foot soldiers and thousand archers

15. From the region of Poitou

and crossbowmen, the Englisc were in for a weighty encounter. By now, everything was in place, and the bloody ceremony could begin. And that's precisely when that crazy Taillefer surprised us all.

*

After consultations with the duke, Taillefer rushed forth on his horse, crossed the plain so fast that, in no time, he reached the rapid ascent towards Senlac, thrusting forwards directly towards the enemy. Mid-slope, he veered leftwards, knocked down an Englisc and chopped off his head, which rolled in a vermilion spurt. The madman returned towards us, very probably saved by the general stupefaction, "Come on! What are you waiting for? Strike!"

The duke raised his rod of command.

"Dex aïe[16]!" Upon this cry, we launched our uphill assault, covered by our archers who fired clouds of arrows in high shots, forcing the enemy to raise its shields. From the third line of foot soldiers that progressed towards the plateau, I could hear the Englisc bellowing "Out! Out!"

Aooouuuttt! Aooouuuttt! A shower of javelins,

---

16. War cry meaning "May god help!"

batons and axes shattered lives. My shield exploded. The tentacles of fear were strangling me, my stomach was in my mouth. Our cavalry drove forward to cover us, but came face to face with the enemy wall. Our decimated lines retreated like fear-stricken ants, whilst the most hideous of smells exuded from the battlefield: the pungent smell of blood, of bodies discharging their abominable liquid. A dying man, his throat ripped open, silently implored me. Dead soldiers, all around! Everywhere, the entangled bodies of horses, shattered weapons, shrieks of pain. A bodiless arm protruded from a bush. I slipped in a pool of red mud. I...

How long did I lay there, my nose in the oily grass, with sparks in my eyes? A powerful hand helped me back up. It was Erwin! Standing, dazed, I noticed that the left wing had taken over. In turn, it was shattered and dispersed by the wall of Englisc shields.

"Run!"

Just like the other hundreds of men around us, Erwin took to his heels, with the enemy on his tail. An unpleasant sensation behind my back. I turned round: three Englisc soldiers were diving towards me, their swords raised. I sliced one of them from head to tail. As the second tried to circumvent, I plunged Chopper into his thigh. The third grazed my arm, but his guard was too low. In a lightning cut, I broke his back. Now, run! Fear pounded, rout resounded. Run! I escaped the carnage, plunging amidst a turmoil of foot soldiers and horsemen. I finally looked myself over, covered in bloody earth and vile filth. All around me, I discovered pallid warriors, glistening with dirty sweat, trying to regain their breath. I could see one looking, staggered, at the two remaining fingers on his left hand. Then William's voice resounded,

"Reform the ranks!"

A javelin whistled by. William's black horse collapsed. The duke rolled on the ground, out of my sight.

"William is dead!" exclaimed a chorus of voices.

*

Impossible. I drove my way through the mass of runaways. I searched. There! On the ground, the duke. He stood up and asked a Manceau to lend him his mount, but I could tell the coward was preparing to flee. I leapt forward, in a vengeful surge, bringing down the horseman who sprawled in the mud.

"At your service, sire duke."

Despite his fleeing troops and his aching back, William managed to smile at me. He mounted the horse.

"Your name?" he enquired.

I told him, upon which he raised his helmet and bellowed that he was alive. Odo, Eustace of Boulogne and others joined him. Together, we strove to stop the absconders in their tracks. The flood of fear ebbed away and the duke spurred courage the length and breadth of the remaining lines. Late morning, the battle could resume.

*

At the foot of the hill, we encircled several hundred Englisc soldiers. Kill! Kill! I was no more than a ball of fire, of force, of folly. I beat, I brought down, I was no longer really aware of what I was doing, but I did it. Squirts of blood, shattered shields, split helmets. There was an ever-increasing empty circle around me. "Hey!" said a familiar voice. Boselin, helmetless, a nasty wound on his forehead, scolded, "Stop it! Can't you see they're dead?"

We joined a group of Norman infantrymen, leaving behind a trail of dead bodies.

Give me strength!

Midday marked a further massacre. The afternoon was hardly any better. Three assaults, three retreats. Haro, and off we went again! Under the ferocious waves of combat and carnage, I was but a pebble among pebbles, driven by the strong surging current. This time, the fury of the waters propelled me to the top of the plateau. Shields tumbled in front of me. Chopper reaped her harvest. But the battle was not yet won, for amidst the torment, looming giants of iron slaughtered anyone who dared cross their path, in a gust of wild axes. The Danes! Who would dare claim to look them in the eye without a blade opening their skulls to the teeth? Yet I challenged them, my courage whipped up by pallid terror. May the souls of my ancestors give me strength! The first Dane curled up, as Chopper flayed his entrails. Then a second. Die! And a third. With his shield, he forcefully fended me off. Twice, his axe grazed my hauberk. I managed a feint, my veins pulsating with horror. The shield hit me again, straight in the chest.

I was dizzy, I could feel my legs weaken under my excessively heavy body. The Danish axe rose. And fell.
Adieu.

Splinters of ice

All around, stench and groans. I was lying in a tent, among the damned as they implored God, as they called for their mothers. I was lapsing into the void.

*

I resurfaced. Ditbert was leaning over me, Godfré behind him, smiling.
"Don't move Squirrel. You've been nastily stunned by the back of a Danish axe, but thankfully for your pins, you were lucky enough to roll down the hill. Praise God for his clemency... and praise your little legs for jumping back so deftly."
Perhaps. But something else made me fret.
"Erwin... Do you know what's become of him?"
"He's dead," replied Godfré, his voice barely audible.
Splinters of ice in my chest.
"God will welcome him among the brave," Ditbert added, convinced he was consoling

me. "He fell along with Turgis. But Taillefer is singing as loud as ever and Boselin is getting blind drunk.

...

Don't you want to know the rest, Squirrel?"

The rest! Without Gwenaël, without Erwin... What did I care.

"Stop looking so forlorn. Victory is ours and the traitor has breathed his last breath. If that's not good news?"

"Fantastic. I can go home to Normandy."

"Out of the question!" (Ditbert's nose protruded and quivered like a beetroot in the wind).

"Excuse me, but I really don't feel like laughing."

"You're going to have to force yourself: the duke has appointed you as a member of his guard."

"Me. Why me?"

"And he wants to know why! Ah, I really like you, you know!" (He leaned over me, hugged me and cried – yes, Ditbert cried!)

November 1066

Mahaut, my dearest sweetheart, if you could see me, you wouldn't recognise your Arnoul! Everyone speaks to me with respect and I don the richest attire. I am advancing towards London, at William's side. Yet, in my slumber, I can still see the battlefield at Hastings and, every night, I am overwhelmed with fear.
Will your kisses ever heal me?

DOCUMENTARY NOTEBOOK

1066: an eventful year...

5th January: death of the English King Edward the Confessor.

6th January: Harold Godwinson is crowned King of England.

24th April: Halley's Comet passes over Normandy.

Throughout the summer: the Norman expeditionary corps gathers in the Dives estuary.

12th September: William moves his army to Saint-Valéry in the Bay of Somme.

20th September: the King of Norway's army lands and defeats the Anglo-Saxons at Fulford.

25th September: King Harold crushes the Norwegians at Stamford Bridge. The King of Norway is killed.

29th September: William's troops land in Pevensey.

14th October: William defeats the English at Battle, near Hastings. Harold is killed.

25th December: William is crowned King of England at Westminster Abbey.

The pretenders...

On 5th January 1066, the King of England, Edward the Confessor, died at the age of 62. His hesitant stance cast doubt over the question of his succession. Several candidates could make a claim to the throne:

- Edgar the Ætheling, born in 1052, grandson to King Edmund II; his young age and lack of political support belittled the seriousness of his claim compared to other pretenders.

- Harold Godwinson, born circa 1022, Earl of Wessex, chief of the aristocracy in southern England, the deceased king's brother-in-law. He was of great influence and Edward may well have designated him as his successor from his death bed.

- William the Bastard, born circa 1027, Duke of Normandy since 1035. Cousin of the recently deceased king who is said to have promised his succession, in 1051 then in 1064, as portrayed in the Bayeux Tapestry.

- Harald Sigurdson (Hardrada), born circa 1015, King of Norway since 1046 after having fought for Byzantium. He claimed the English throne following an old agreement between the English and Norwegian kings. Tostig, Harold's estranged brother, allied with him.

- Sweyn of Denmark, born circa 1029, King of Denmark since 1047. He tried to capture England later, in 1069 and 1074.

On 6th January 1066, an assembly of English noblemen, called the *Witeganemot*, proposed the crown to Harold Godwinson. He accepted despite the oath he had sworn to William during his travels to Normandy in 1064. He was immediately crowned King of England. William decided to cross the English Channel. Harald Hardrada, the King of Norway, also led an expedition to invade England from the north.

William and
the others...

William the Bastard was born around 1027 from the love of the Norman Duke Robert and beautiful Herleva of Falaise. His duchy, home to around 700,000 inhabitants, was a prosperous one. William married the Count of Flanders' daughter, Matilda. He was cousin to Edward, the King of England, who is said to have promised him his throne; however, after the king's death, Harold Godwinson was crowned. The duke set off to conquer England, with moral support from the Pope.

Among his faithful companions: his two brothers, Odo, bishop of Bayeux, and Robert of Mortain, the Seneschal FitzOsbern, Roger de Montgomerie, William de Warenne, Roger de Beaumont... along with a few ecclesiastics, among whom Lanfranc. The duke's vassals provided him with ships and the necessary troops for his expedition. Meanwhile, Montgomerie and Beaumont helped Matilda to rule over Normandy. In 1067, Odo and FitzOsbern governed the kingdom during William's return to Normandy.

Not because he was tall, our William, but because of the determination that glistened in his grey eyes, his hostile expression, his mouth, deliberately indented with a short nose and a powerful chin, conveying a rare strength of character. *Detail from the Bayeux Tapestry, 11th century.*

Harold and the others...

Before heading back to England, Harold swore an oath of allegiance to our duke on holy relics. *Detail from the Bayeux Tapestry, 11th century.*

The kingdom of England, home to around 1,500,000 inhabitants, was independent and unified since 954; however, it went through a period of alternating Anglo-Saxon and Danish kings over the 10th and 11th centuries. Harold succeeded his father in 1053 as Earl of Wessex (representing a third of England!), hence becoming the most powerful English lord after the king. In 1064, after shipwrecking off the Ponthieu coast, Harold was placed in the hands of Duke William of Normandy, who obtained from him an oath to help William accede to the English throne. In 1065, Harold offered support to the Northumbrian rebellion raised against his brother Tostig. The latter sought refuge with the King of Norway. Upon Edward's death, the Witenagemot designated Harold as his successor. However, Harald and Tostig soon landed and defeated the English at the Battle of Fulford. Harold then took the Norwegians by surprise at Stamford Bridge where both Harald and Tostig were killed. On the 14th of October 1066, Harold's army, weakened despite the presence of fearsome housecarls, challenged the Normans near Hastings.

States and places

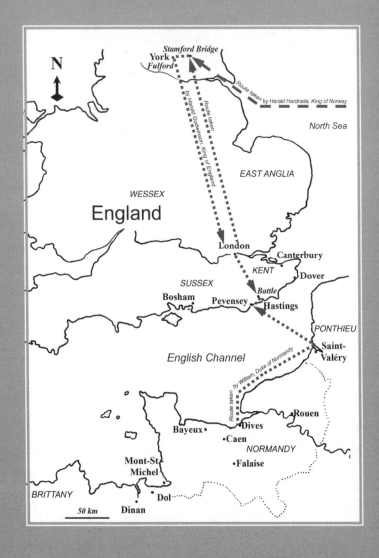

Preparations

The invasion project

The Duke of Normandy was quick to react. He needed an armada capable of transporting, not only men of arms, but also their horses. Ships were hastily built in the ports of Normandy. When William consulted his barons, they all agreed to provide the duke with a certain number of vessels: his brothers first - one hundred ships from Odo and one hundred and twenty from Robert; his other important vassals each promised between sixty and eighty. According to the historian Pierre Bouet, the total fleet could be estimated at around a thousand ships. The finest of the fleet was undoubtedly *Mora* (Amor/love?), a ship commissioned by Matilda for her husband.

The expeditionary corps

William also raised an army to lead an exhibition outside the frontiers of his duchy. The duke progressively negotiated with his vassals to obtain their adhesion for the feudal ost consisted of forty days' service. The Normans were joined by mercenaries from Brittany and Flanders. The "Bastard's" army comprised between seven and eight thousand men including between two thousand and two thousand five hundred well-trained horsemen and three to six thousand horses. The horsemen's prowess, associated with that of the archers, was to do wonders at Hastings.

The time has come for the waves of adventure, and of war.
Detail from the Bayeux Tapestry, 11th century.

Assembly at Dives

William reunited his expeditionary corps in the Dives estuary, which was a genuine gulf at the time of his reign. Roger de Montgomerie, a local lord and one of the duke's advisers, very probably played an active role in preparing the expedition, even if he remained in Normandy to help the duchess, Matilda. Harold expected William to land in the south of England; however, the Bastard hoped for strong winds to take his fleet further north. Yet, the southerly wind was only to facilitate the departure of Harald's Norwegian troops. This proved to be a godsend for William, for he was to face an enemy already exhausted by its long travels and diminished during the harsh battle at Stamford Bridge. On the 12th of September, William changed his base and took his fleet to Saint-Valery in the Bay of Somme. Then, he crossed the English Channel by night to land in Pevensey on the morning of the 29th of September, without encountering the slightest hostility, for Harold was busy in the north.

The forces present on the morning of 14th October 1066

After landing, the Norman army entrenched itself in Hastings. Negotiations then began between the two rivals... In vain. On the 13th of October, Harold's troops took up positions on the top of a hill, since named Battle Hill, located to the north of Hastings. On the morning of the 14th, Harold positioned his men, all foot soldiers, to form a front of a width of around two thousand six hundred feet. On the front line, he placed his elite soldiers, the two thousand housecarls armed with huge Danish axes. Behind them, the second line and side ranks comprised the six thousand hastily requisitioned fyrd peasants, who formed several lines. Harold took up position to the rear.

Opposite them, at arrow-firing distance, William's army occupied an two thousand six hundred feet-long front at the foot of the hill upon which the English were camped. The French and Flemish troops occupied the right wing, positioned to the northeast, whilst the Normans were in the centre and the Bretons on the left wing, to the southwest. A thousand archers and crossbowmen were positioned in the front line, the second line comprising of four thousand foot soldiers armed with spikes and javelins. Finally, two thousand to two thousand five hundred horsemen formed the rear. Duke William established his command post immediately behind his troops on the slopes of Telham Hill. It was a spot from which he could intervene, whatever the turn of events.

It is of traditional belief that, at the start of the battle, a horseman and troubadour named Ivo Taillefer rode at great speed towards the enemy declaiming the first lines of *the Song of Roland*.

The course of the Battle of Hastings [14th October 1066]

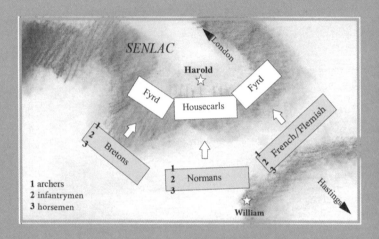

1. **Around 9 am:** the two armies were face to face. The English troops formed a compact "wall" at the top of Battle Hill. The Normans were below. The direction of their arrows proved ineffective; the assault by the cavalry, whose momentum was broken by the slope of the hill, met with the "wall" of English shields.

Detail from the Bayeux Tapestry, 11th century.

Our cavalry drove forward to cover us,
but came face to face with the enemy wall.

Detail from the Bayeux Tapestry, 11th century.

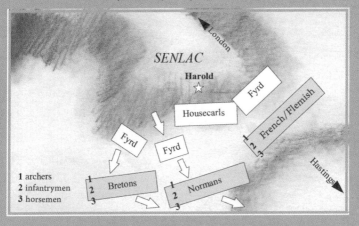

2. At around midday, the Bretons from the left wing yielded, leading to the withdrawal of the Normans in the centre, then the Franco-Flemish to the right. William intervened, but his horse was killed from under him. Immediately, a rumour spread, "William is dead!" resulting in an instant and frantic retreat. However, the duke got back up onto his feet and took another horse. He directly raised his helmet and turned towards his men to prevent them from routing. Meanwhile, the English had left their positions. Much to their misfortune, for the Norman cavalry charged, then encircled and exterminated them.

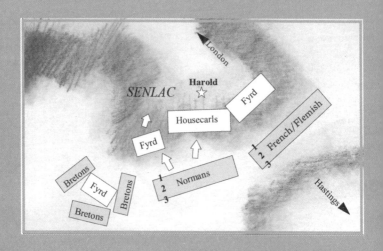

3. **In the afternoon**, groups of Harold's soldiers left their ranks once more to attack the Normans, who feigned retreat. And each time they did so, their assailants were massacred. Harold's army was consequently plunged into chaos. Over the morning, Harold had already lost his two brothers, Gyrth and Leofwine.

After sustained fire by the Norman archers, the infantry resumed its assault, surprising the wings of the English ranks. **At around 4pm**, perhaps already wounded in the eye by an arrow, Harold was attacked and killed by four horsemen. With no chief, the English chaotically withdrew, whilst attempting desperate skirmishes here and there. Although the outcome was for a long time unsure, thanks to the skilful use of his cavalry, William won the battle.

A few years later, King William had Battle Abbey built. The church's high altar was placed on the exact spot where Harold was killed.

The Norman
conquest of England

From Hastings to Westminster

By the evening of the 14th of October 1066, the Duke of
Normandy is said to have lost a third of his army, his remaining
forces amounting to 1,960 horsemen and 3,720 infantrymen...
Over the weeks that followed, William conquered Dover,
then Canterbury, continuing towards Winchester, without –
as yet – attacking London. Stigand had just surrendered in
Wallingford, soon to be followed by Ætheling Edgar, the last
born of the Anglo-Saxon royal family, then by the kingdom's
leading noblemen. They all swore allegiance to William, who
accepted the crown, but, before entering London, ordered the
construction of a fortification that was to become the Tower
of London.

William the king

William the Conqueror was crowned King of England on
Christmas Day 1066 in the abbey-church of Westminster;
however, upon hearing the cries from the crowd as they
acclaimed their new king, the Norman guards feared a riot
and set fire to the nearby houses. William still needed to
conquer the hearts of all his new subjects...

After 1066, England turned to Western Europe, whereas
Normandy, whose power had been multiplied, became a
mortal danger for the kingdom of France, but that's another
story...

Sources

BOÜARD (de) Michel, *Guillaume le Conquérant*, Éditions Fayard.

BOUET Pierre, *Guillaume le Conquérant et les Normands au xı^e siècle*, Éditions Charles Corlet.

BOUET Pierre, *Hastings 14 octobre 1066*, Éditions Texto.

CARPENTIER Vincent, *Guillaume le Conquérant et l'estuaire de la Dives*, Éditions de l'Association Le Pays d'Auge.

GONDOIN Stéphane, MOGÈRE S. et DAVRIL, *Chroniques anglo-saxonnes, 1. L'Angleterre normande*, Assor BD.

GRAVETT Christopher, *Hastings 1066*, Osprey History.

GRAVETT Christopher et Hook Christa, *Norman Knight*, Osprey History.

NEVEUX François, *Guillaume le Conquérant*, Éditions Ouest France.

RIDEL Élisabeth, *Les Navires de la Conquête*, OREP Éditions.

Contents

Dans la même collection

LES ÉRABLES DE SANG
Juno Beach - 6 juin 1944

- Patrick BOUSQUET-SCHNEEWEIS et Michel GIARD
- Format : 130 x 210 mm
- 80 pages intérieures
- Couverture souple
- Dos carré, collé, cousu
- Langues : français, anglais
- Prix : 7,50 €

– Ici Marcel Ouimet de Radio Canada. Je me trouve avec les hommes du régiment de la Chaudière devant une petite station balnéaire nommée Bernières-sur-Mer. Des tirs d'obus en provenance des batteries allemandes s'intensifient autour de nous ! L'ordre de l'assaut est enfin donné ! J'imagine l'émotion de nos valeureux soldats en ces instants historiques car, pour beaucoup, dans leurs veines, coule du sang français...
De Montréal à Juno Beach, l'incroyable odyssée des Canadiens qui, le 6 juin 1944, nous ont aidés à recouvrer notre liberté...

LES FANTÔMES DE PORT-WINSTON
Arromanches - 6 juin 1944

- Patrick BOUSQUET-SCHNEEWEIS et Michel GIARD
- Format : 130 x 210 mm
- 80 pages intérieures
- Couverture souple
- Dos carré, collé, cousu
- Langues : français, anglais
- Prix : 7,50 €

La vision des vestiges des pontons d'Arromanches embua de larmes les yeux de Julie, qui ne put s'empêcher de frissonner. Les spectres, qu'elle avait pensé exorciser en faisant le voyage jusqu'ici, étaient de retour. Plus présents que jamais...
De la construction du port artificiel d'Arromanches au massacre de la prison de Caen, le matin même du Débarquement, retrouvez les fantômes qui hantent aujourd'hui encore Port-Winston.

UNE PLAGE EN ENFER
Omaha Beach - 6 juin 1944

- Patrick BOUSQUET-SCHNEEWEIS et Michel GIARD
- Format : 130 x 210 mm
- 80 pages intérieures
- Couverture souple
- Dos carré, collé, cousu
- Langues : français, anglais
- Prix : 7,50 €

Je m'appelle William Bishop. J'appartiens à la 1re division d'infanterie américaine, la fameuse « Big Red One ». Nous sommes le 6 juin 1944 et, dans quelques minutes, je vais débarquer sur la plage d'Omaha la sanglante... Voici mon histoire...

LES DIABLES DE PEGASUS
Pont de Bénouville - 6 juin 1944

- Patrick BOUSQUET-SCHNEEWEIS et Michel GIARD
- Format : 130 x 210 mm
- 72 pages intérieures
- Couverture souple
- Dos carré, collé, cousu
- Langues : français, anglais
- Prix : 7,50 €

Dans le planeur n° 1, les soldats se tenaient par le bras dans l'attente du formidable choc qui ne manquerait pas de se produire lorsque l'avion prendrait contact avec le sol.
Peu après, le Horsa laboura la terre dans une pluie d'étincelles avant de finir sa course à proximité des barbelés qui entouraient le pont.
– Tout le monde dehors ! Grouillez-vous, les gars ! hurla un officier en bondissant de l'appareil...
Partagez l'histoire de la prise du pont de Bénouville avec les hommes de la 6e division aéroportée britannique dans la nuit du 5 au 6 juin 1944.

GO ! GERONIMO !
Sainte-Mère-Église - 6 juin 1944

- Patrick BOUSQUET-SCHNEEWEIS et Michel GIARD
- Format : 130 x 210 mm
- 80 pages intérieures
- Couverture souple
- Dos carré, collé, cousu
- Langues : français, anglais
- Prix : 7,50 €

« Steve, qui devait être le premier à franchir la porte du C-47, sentit son cœur battre la chamade. Cette fois, il n'était plus question de reculer.
– Go !, fit le largueur en lui tapant sur l'épaule.
– Geronimo !, s'écria Barrow en plongeant dans le vide obscur de la nuit.
Très vite, le ciel de Normandie se constella de centaines de corolles... »
Revivez la formidable épopée des paras de la 82e aéroportée qui sautèrent sur Sainte-Mère-Église dans la nuit du 5 au 6 juin 1944...

LES ÉTOILES DE LA LIBERTÉ
Utah Beach - 6 juin 1944

- Patrick BOUSQUET-SCHNEEWEIS et Michel GIARD
- Format : 130 x 210 mm
- 80 pages intérieures
- Couverture souple
- Dos carré, collé, cousu
- Langues : français, anglais
- Prix : 7,50 €

Slapton Sands ! Une plage anglaise de sinistre mémoire pour tous ceux qui, comme le capitaine Schroeder, en avril 1944, avaient participé à l'opération *Tiger*, la tragique répétition du débarquement en Normandie.
Deux mois plus tard, à Utah Beach, Schroeder et ses hommes étaient bien décidés à venger la mort de leurs camarades...
À travers l'histoire de Leonard Schroeder, suivez l'épopée des soldats américains qui, le 6 juin 1944, ont recouvert les ténèbres de cinq années d'occupation sous une myriade d'étoiles. Les étoiles de la Liberté...

In the same collection

THE BLOODY MAPLES
Juno Beach - June 6th 1944

- Patrick BOUSQUET-SCHNEEWEIS and Michel GIARD
- Format: 130 x 210mm
- 80 inside pages
- Soft cover
- Square back, sewn, pasted
- Language: French, English
- Retail price: €7,50

– 'Marcel Ouimet from Radio Canada here. I am with men from the Régiment de La Chaudière in the small seaside resort of Bernières-sur-Mer. Shellfire from the German artillery batteries is intensifying all around us! The order is finally given to attack! I can imagine the emotion felt by our troops during these historic moments, for many of them have French blood in them…'

From Montreal to Juno Beach, the incredible Canadian odyssey which, on the 6th of June 1944, contributed towards our newfound freedom...

THE GHOSTS OF PORT-WINSTON
Arromanches - June 6th 1944

- Patrick BOUSQUET-SCHNEEWEIS and Michel GIARD
- Format: 130 x 210mm
- 80 inside pages
- Soft cover
- Square back, sewn, pasted
- Language: French, English
- Retail price: €7,50

The image of the ruins of Arromanches' artificial port brought tears to Julie's eyes and she began to shudder involuntarily. The ghosts she thought she had exorcised by coming here had returned. And she felt their presence stronger than ever...

From the construction of Arromanches' artificial port to the Caen prison massacre on the morning of D-Day, meet the ghosts which continue to haunt Port Winston today.

THE BEACH TO HELL
Omaha Beach - June 6th 1944

- Patrick BOUSQUET-SCHNEEWEIS and Michel GIARD
- Format: 130 x 210mm
- 80 inside pages
- Soft cover
- Square back, sewn, pasted
- Language: French, English
- Retail price: €7,50

My name is William Bishop. I belong to the US 1st Infantry Division, the famous Big Red One. Today is the 6th of June 1944 and, in a few minutes, I'll be landing on Omaha Beach, in the Easy Red sector. A beach that will go down in History as Bloody Omaha... This is my story...

THE DEVILS OF PEGASUS
Bénouville Bridge - June 6th 1944

- Patrick BOUSQUET-SCHNEEWEIS and Michel GIARD
- Format: 130 x 210mm
- 72 inside pages
- Soft cover
- Square back, sewn, pasted
- Language: French, English
- Retail price: €7,50

In glider n° 1, the soldiers were braced arm-in-arm ready for the huge impact of the aircraft hitting the ground. There was a deafening noise as the Horsa ploughed the ground in a shower of sparks before coming to a stop by the barbed wire fence surrounding the bridge. 'Everyone out! Move it lads!' yelled an officer as he leapt out of the glider… Join the men of the 6th British Airborne Division on their mission to take Bénouville Bridge on the night of the 5th - 6th of June 1944.

GO! GERONIMO!
Sainte-Mère-Église - June 6th 1944

- Patrick BOUSQUET-SCHNEEWEIS and Michel GIARD
- Format: 130 x 210mm
- 80 inside pages
- Soft cover
- Square back, sewn, pasted
- Language: French, English
- Retail price: €7,50

"Steve, who was to be the first to jump through the door of the C-47, could feel his heart beating like a drum. No danger of turning back this time. "Go!" the dispatcher yelled as he tapped him on the shoulder. "Geronimo!" cried Barrow as he plunged into the dark of the night. The Normandy skies were soon to be illuminated by hundreds of garlands..." Relive the epic feat of the 82nd Airborne paratroopers who jumped out over Sainte-Mère-Église on the night of the 5th to the 6th of June 1944...

THE STARS OF LIBERTY
Utah Beach - June 6th 1944

- Patrick BOUSQUET-SCHNEEWEIS and Michel GIARD
- Format: 130 x 210mm
- 80 inside pages
- Soft cover
- Square back, sewn, pasted
- Language: French, English
- Retail price: €7,50

Slapton Sands! The English beach holds dark memories for those who, like Captain Schroeder, took part in operation *Tiger* in April 1944, the rehearsal of the Normandy landings which ended in tragedy. Two months later, on Utah Beach, Schroeder and his men are determined to avenge the death of their fellow soldiers...

Through Leonard Schroeder's story, follow the journey of American soldiers who, on the 6th of June 1944, put an end to the darkness of five years of occupation with a sea of stars. The stars of Liberty…

Photographic credits

Cover illustration: Arnaud GAUMET
Illustrations p. 66, 67, 70, 72, 73: Details from the Bayeux Tapestry, 11th century, courtesy of the town of Bayeux.
Historic and educational content: Gilles PIVARD
Narration and text : Pierre EFRATAS

ISBN: 978-2-8151-0244-5

© Éditions OREP 2015